Airick Flies High

Written By
Eric Gaffney

Illustrated By
Alisha Wenaas

26 25 24 23 22 21   9 8 7 6 5 4 3 2 1

AIRICK FLIES HIGH
Copyright ©2021 Surefly Writing, LLC

All rights reserved. Except as permitted under the U.S. Copyright Act of 1976, no part of this publication may be reproduced, distributed, or transmitted in any form by any means, or stored in a database or retrieval system, without the prior written permission of the author and/or publisher. Printed in the United States.

Published by:
Emerge Publishing, LLC
2109 E. 69th Street Tulsa, OK 74137
Phone: 888.407.4447   www.Emerge.pub

Library of Congress Cataloging-in-Publication Data:
ISBN: 978-1-954966-03-1 Paperback

BISAC:
JUV041010   JUVENILE FICTION / Transportation / Aviation
JUV039150   JUVENILE FICTION / Disabilities & Special Needs

Illustrations: Alisha Wenaas

Author Contact:
Website: www. ericgaffney.com

Printed in the United States of America

For my parents, Jim and Lori, who always

encouraged me and never treated me differently.

For my wife, Natalie, for loving me and always being there for me.

And for every kid. May you dream big and fly high!

Philippians 4:13

—Eric

For my husband, Jake, for always believing in me

even when I didn't believe in myself.

For my children, may this inspire you to chase your dreams.

—Alisha

In the town of Surefly an airplane named Airick lived in Hanger 301.

The day he had been waiting for was finally here.
It was his first day of flight school and Airick was nervous.

Airick's right wing was
shorter than his left wing.

He was made this way and
he knew he was different.

Because he was not like every other
plane in his class, Airick was afraid that
the other planes would make fun of him.

On his first day of flight school,
Airick's mom and dad told him not to be afraid.
They were excited for him to meet new friends.

Airick tried to be excited.
He believed in himself.
But he was still nervous.

When Airick arrived at the flight school, he began to notice the other planes staring at his shorter wing. Some planes even made mean jokes.

He found his spot for class and
was glad that it was off to the side.

That night Airick told his parents all about his first day. It wasn't all bad. After all, he liked his new teacher.

He even made a new friend named Windy.

As the school year went by,
Airick and his classmates
learned all about how to fly.

Every airplane in his class
would practice different skills.

Some of these skills were hard to learn.
Airick told his parents that he wished
he had two wings that were the same size.
He felt it would make it much easier.

Airick's parents told him he could do it.
If he tried hard enough he could
accomplish anything. Airick knew he could.
He would just need a lot of practice.

Airick did practice a lot.
He practiced before school.
He practiced after school.

He even practiced at school during recess when all the other planes were playing games.

One day Airick was having trouble with one of his lessons.

All the other planes could take-off and make a quick turn to the right.

Airick could not turn as fast as the other planes. He was nervous that he would never fly as well as them.

One thing was certain;
Airick would never give up.
He knew if he kept on trying
he would figure it out.

Airick did figure it out.
He needed to lean a little
harder to make that turn.

Before long, Airick was
completing his lessons
just like the other planes.

Finally the day that every plane had been waiting for had arrived- test day at Surefly Flight School.

It was time for all the planes in Airick's class to demonstrate their flying skills. Like all the other planes, Airick was nervous, but he knew he was ready.

He wanted to go first.

Airick was ready for this day.
He had practiced a lot and worked very hard.
His friend, Windy, wished him good luck
before the test.

SUCCESS!!

Airick passed his flight test!
His mom and dad were there
to congratulate him.

That day Airick was given a ribbon for "High Achiever."

He was very proud of himself.

Airick was thrilled. He had always been told he could do anything if he believed in himself. And now he couldn't wait to show it!

Eric Gaffney - Author

Eric Gaffney, a Broken Arrow, OK native, was born without his right hand. He attended the University of Oklahoma, where he graduated with a professional pilot degree. The challenges that Airick faces in *Airick Flies High* represent the challenges Eric had to overcome in his career.

Through constant perseverance, Eric is now a 737 pilot for United Airlines. He lives in Broken Arrow with his wife, Natalie, their two children, Cameron and Austin, and their dog, Daisy. **Contact Eric Gaffney at SureflyWriting@gmail.com**

Alisha Wenaas - Illustrator

Alisha Wenaas has had a passion for art from an early age. She studied art in high school and has taken art courses at her local community college, but is primarily self-taught, learning through experience. She hopes to inspire children to pursue their creative passions through any means possible, formal or informal, like she did as a young girl.

She works primarily with oil paints from her home in Barnsdall, OK, where she lives with her husband, Jake, and their three children.

Made in the USA
Las Vegas, NV
22 May 2022